FIND OUT ABOUT
GLASS

This edition 2002

© Franklin Watts 1994

Franklin Watts
96 Leonard Street
LONDON EC2A 4XD

Franklin Watts Australia
45-51 Huntley Street
Alexandria
NSW 2015

ISBN: 0 7496 4775 2

Dewey Decimal Classification 666

A CIP catalogue record for this book
is available from the British Library

Editor: Annabel Martin
Design: Thumb Design
Cover Design: Chloe Cheesman
Cover Stained Glass: Judith Sovin
Picture Research: Alison Renwick

Additional photographs:
Ancient Art & Architecture Collection
© Ronald Sheridon 5; Courtesy of
Pilkington Glass 8, 9; T. Hill 19, 24;
© Sonia Halliday & Laura Lushington 29;
Courtesy of United Glass 10.

Printed in Hong Kong, China

FIND OUT ABOUT
GLASS

Henry Pluckrose

Photography by Chris Fairclough

W
FRANKLIN WATTS
LONDON•SYDNEY

These containers are called glasses.
Can you think why?

A method of making glass
was discovered by the Ancient Egyptians
about 3000 years ago.
This glass bowl is very old.

Glass is made by mixing
sand and limestone
with chemicals.
The mixture is heated
until it melts.

While it is still hot
the mixture is blown into shape.
The glassblower blows down the pipe.
The hot glass expands –
just like a balloon.

Today most glass is made
in factories called glassworks.
The mixture of sand, limestone
and soda ash
is heated in a large furnace
until it is red hot.

To make flat sheets of glass
the red hot mixture
is poured into a bath.
The bath contains liquid tin.
The liquid glass spreads out
on the tin
to make a thin sheet.

To make bottles and jars
the hot glass is poured
into a mould.
A machine blows air
into the mould.

The air pushes the liquid glass against the sides of the mould to make the bottle.
An empty space is left inside it. Light bulbs are made in this way.

Glass can be used in many different ways. It is strong and it keeps out wind and rain. We use it for windows.

This picture was taken
through a glass window.
Glass is transparent –
we can see through it.
Glass windows let sunlight
into our homes, schools and offices.

A person who cuts
and fits glass
is called a glazier.

A glazier cuts glass to size with a special tool.
Its cutting edge is made from a tiny diamond.

Sheet glass is used for shop windows and greenhouses. In the summer the sun's heat is trapped in the greenhouse. The warmth helps plants to grow more quickly.

Special glass is used for
the windcreens of buses,
cars and lorries.
If this glass is smashed
it does not splinter.
Why are windscreens
made with this glass?

Glass has a smooth surface which is easy to clean. It is used to make bottles and jars for food and drink.

Glass does not burn.
It will not rot away.
Containers made of glass
are used to store chemicals.

Many household items
are made of glass.

Some bowls and dishes
are made of heat-resistant glass.
They will not crack if they are used
as cooking pots.

Glass is used in the home
for many other things –
for ornaments,
trinket boxes and paperweights,
and also in the faces of clocks.

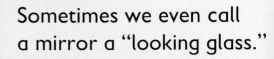

Sometimes we even call a mirror a "looking glass."

Glass is used by scientists
in their laboratories.
Glass can be shaped
into thin pipes, hollow tubes
and strangely shaped containers.

Lenses made of glass
are used in microscopes.
A microscope is a tool
which makes it possible
to see very small objects
by magnifying them.

The special glass used in microscopes
is called optic glass.
Optic glass is also used
to make the lenses
in spectacles.

Where would you find
the optic glass in these things?

Glass is also used by craftsmen and women. The engraver has cut a design into the surface of this vase.

This artist is using coloured glass to make a picture. The pieces of glass are held together with strips of lead.

This is a stained glass window
in a church.
It was made hundreds of years ago.

Brown   Clear   Green

KEEP DEVON SHIPSHAPE

LASS BOTTLES AND JARS

ottle Banks are operated by Devon County Council with your local District Council

116

Every day we use something
made of glass.
Things made of glass
can be recycled.
Is there a bottle bank
near your home?
Does your family use it?

About this book

This book is designed for use in the home, kindergarten and infant school.

Parents can share the book with young children. Its aim is to bring into focus some of the elements of life and living which are all too often taken for granted. To develop fully, all young children need to have their understanding of the world deepened and the language they use to express their ideas extended. This book, and others in the series, takes the everyday things of the child's world and explores them, harnessing curiosity and wonder in a purposeful way.

For those working with young children each book is designed to be used both as a picture book, which explores ideas and concepts and as a starting point to talk and exploration. The pictures have been selected because they are of interest in themselves and also because they include elements which will promote enquiry. Talk can lead to displays of items and pictures collected by children and teacher. Pictures and collages can be made by the children themselves.

Everything in our environment is of interest to the growing child. The purpose of these books is to extend and develop that interest.

Henry Pluckrose